THE REAL SUBJECT

KEITH WALDROP ■ ■ ■ ■ ■ ■ ■ ■

THE REAL

Omnidawn   Richmond, California   2004

SUBJECT

QUERIES AND CONJECTURES OF JACOB DELAFON

■ ■ ■ ■ ■ ■ ■ WITH SAMPLE POEMS

$\overline{\text{O}}_{\text{MNIDAWN}}$

Richmond, California
www.omnidawn.com
(800) 792-4957

Copyright © 2004 by Keith Waldrop
All rights reserved
Printed in the United States
on acid-free recycled paper

ISBN 1-890650-15-3

Cover collage by Keith Waldrop
Cover design by Quemadura

Cataloging-in-Publication Data appear at the end of the book

dedicated to
Raymond Ragosta

J.D. / K.W.

*There are songs which need,
for orchestration, only the wind.*

LEOS JANACEK

Jacob Delafon reads: "To treat a fever, cut a cockchafer in two. Tape half of it to your right arm and the other half to your left."

He wonders about this.

What, actually, is a "cockchafer"? — he finds it a disturbing term.

He looks it up. It is a "pale-brown nocturnal beetle flying with a loud whirring sound."

All this is theoretical. Jacob has no fever.

■

Jacob Delafon reads, somewhere, that all human activity lies along two opposing vectors: the centrifugal push of paranoia and the centripetal pull of hysteria.

■

Jacob Delafon has read of a debate among doctors, as to

whether nuns or prostitutes are more susceptible to hysteria.

■

Jacob Delafon locates the word *orthoepy*, meaning the "correct pronunciation of words." The word seems to him unpronounceable.

■

Jacob Delafon, noting that Parsifal (like his cousin Lancelot) is a descendant of Joseph of Arimathea who, in turn, is of the House of David—in short, that Parsifal is a Jew—wonders if Wagner was aware of this.

WHIR

do not alarm yourself, I
could not rest content with
moral lectures and continual
repetition

like the solar system, I
could not hold my head up, made
endlessly to
glow

destined for grand ceremonies, I
was much affected by finding myself so
thin and so worn
down

(we use theory
to mean it is possible to
choose, e.g., why I am just the
size I am)

a million million, a
cool and mortifying manner—what
governs
motion

Jacob Delafon reads *A la recherche du temps perdu*.

In the last pages of the last volume, he finds the Past has been recaptured. The teeming World (i.e., the Novel) is now reduced to a single Character.

This must be, Jacob considers, hysteria's major text.

■

Jacob Delafon is surprised to read of ancient astronomers who "defied Time."

Later, he realizes it is a misprint for *deified*.

■

Time is something Jacob Delafon would prefer not to think about. But it does disturb him that while time seems—*moving image of eternity*—to slide around him somehow on its way elsewhere, at the same time ("Time," he mutters, "there it is again"), appears also completely at rest, standing absolutely still, while he himself plunges, or is plunged, through it.

4

If he reads that time began only with the creation—waste-and-void or big bang—he wonders, What came before? and is appalled how some have supposed we have a completely new space for each tick of elapsed time.

He would like to tear himself from the past. If, that is, he could postpone the future.

He feels the present as time borrowed, a borrowing beyond his means, a debt he can never hope to pay.

He would pay whatever he could to believe that time contradicts itself. He would give anything for a timely miracle.

He craves *an interval*.

He dreams an end of time (but thinks What then?) and tries to believe, as has been claimed, that when the heavenly bodies cease to rotate, then also his soul will cease to yearn.

■

Jacob Delafon comes across the notion of black holes. He finds it hard to believe in anything so singular.

■

Monsieur Teste calls his wife by three pet names:

Être,

Chose,

Oasis.

Jacob Delafon tries to come up with suitable names for his girl friend, Jane Floodcab. He considers

See.

Eat.

Choir.

S. O. S.

■

Jacob Delafon has a nightmare which breaks into frag-ments, each fragment a nightmare on its own, like a worm cut in pieces, each segment still active, wriggling through his troubled sleep.

■

Jacob Delafon is told that, after death, we will know nothing, but pain will continue. He regards this as unwarranted optimism.

■

Left to himself, Jacob Delafon repeats the execration text—which he has by rote—in a version made personal and containing the words *mon coeur et mon corps*.

Invariably he stops short of the riddance ritual.

■

His problem, Jacob Delafon decides, is how not to exist—without losing consciousness.

SINGULAR

have spoilt me (you have) bodies of
planets

angels, forced
to postulate *matter*

asked her (I asked) if she would
like to dance, how
crude we are

composed of ether, of
either

is it for such
insults that I have climbed
all these flights

Is there an adequate reason, Jacob Delafon wonders, for the creation and continuation of the universe?

He—Jacob, I mean—still, you see (naïve), still thinks there is a universe.

■

The historians that Jacob Delafon has read lately seem to him determined to show all the great historical moments (those, at least, that his rather random education has presented him) as false. None of them, he finds—one after another—ever happened.

Luther, it seems, never actually said, "Here I stand ..."

Galileo never climbed the leaning tower of Pisa to drop his balls of wood and iron.

And even *natural* history moves in the same direction, the ostrich never hiding his head in the sand.

■

Jacob Delafon has tried three times to write his memoirs, which he thinks of as a philosophical work. He has never gotten past the first sentence.

The first version started:

So I returned

The second:

Then I returned

And the third:

I returned

■

Jacob Delafon has trouble with his computer. It seems to him that, performing the same operation, he sometimes gets different results. Forced, thus, to speculate that what he is dealing with is not exactly a machine.

■

Mindfulness, Jacob Delafon realizes, is not thoughtfulness.

But he cannot stop this train of thought. Neither, he continues—his ideas, as usual, in flight—is it a white cloak on a floating island. Nor creature of the night: not cat, not bat, not even dream. Not the hatching of plot while underground.

Odd, he thinks, how everything conspires.

Strange renga.

■

I can turn my face to the south.

Or to the north.

I can point my finger upward.

Downward.

Jacob Delafon is impressed by any evidence of free will.

■

Jacob Delafon is unable, despite fervent effort, to forsake images, to move beyond a world of images. He knows, of course, that they distort him, project onto him the shapes of animals. That the deep truth is imageless.

But to nice distinctions, in spite of himself, he still prefers the shadows of resemblance. His most personal cry has a universal sound, like words.

■

The reaction of Jacob Delafon to these various notes can be classified into six types:

positive

negative

oriented

tolerant

playful

hostile

■

Jacob Delafon is fascinated by words William Cowper heard spoken by God, by Satan, or by his own lips:

"all's over with you—you have perished"

"she shall recover"

"she is yours for many years"

"your watch must be wound up again"

"water it with tears and strong cries"

[Dreamed that in a state of the most insupportable misery I looked through the window of a strange room being all alone, and saw preparations making for my execution. That it was but about four days distant, and that then I was destined to suffer everlasting martyrdom in the fire, my body being prepared for the purpose and my dissolution made a thing impossible.]

"I shall perish *which was immediately answered by a vision of a wineglass, and these words,* —

"A whole glass. *In allusion, no doubt, to the famous story of Mrs Honeywood.*"

[Mrs Honeywood, having a wineglass in her hand, cried, "I am as surely damned, as this glass is broken!" flinging the glass to the ground. But the glass did not break.]

"I see in *this* case just occasion of Pity"

13

"... I promise thee much, without fear, and more than thou canst *bear*"

"to be glorious is to be near to Thee, and that glory is mine"

"I will promise you any thing"

"only just to tell you that I am, and that I am with you"

"you understand me right, William"

"the dreadful visit is paid"

■

And he is impressed (Jacob Delafon, that is) by how William Cowper explained to William Blake his own madness, and also Blake's: "mad as a refuge from unbelief."

■

Jacob Delafon picks up *The Sunny Side of Christianity* by Charles H. Parkhurst, a book published in 1901.

The chapter "Love in the Heart versus Phosphorus in the Brain" is disappointing, but Jacob admires another, on "Love Considered as a Lubricant."

INTERVAL

the optimum level of
arousal, where there is
nothing to see

after I
die, deepest and dearest
sorrow—I'll

masquerade, pointing to
various degrees
of substance, until

all tears, other-
wise

Jane Floodcab's attitudes towards Jacob, over a period of time, can be classified as:

negative

tolerant

playful

protective

attaching

■

Jacob Delafon reads that, when painting the portrait of a living creature, it helps first to sketch the bones.

He cannot bring himself to start—Jane Floodcab posed before him—so likely it seems to him that he will never be up to adding vein or sinew, much less clothing the body with flesh and with skin.

■

Jacob Delafon does not claim to have strong senses or deep feeling. What serves him in a way as such is to remember what used to please him long ago, maybe—he thinks, if not careful—thousands of years ago.

■

In the dark, Jacob Delafon finds everything simple. The dark has no distracting surfaces, no inside-and-outside, no layering, nothing deep, nothing *seeming*.

In daylight, amid the dimensions of sight, among so many hidden things, fully hidden, partly hidden, profundities, opacities, mysteries of position and composition, he does not understand anything.

■

At the period when light fades and darkness makes its appearance, then it is, thinks Jacob Delafon, that he should affirm the failing day, the place within which he is not, the nothing in the all.

■

Jacob Delafon is not sure what he thinks of life, but he is used to it.

■

This world, Jacob Delafon hears, is governed by angels.

He checks out a guide to Aquinas, the Angelic Doctor, and reads:

"There is nothing in an angel that might fall out, come loose, or be cut off."

"In their search for the kind of a body they needed, the angels were not reduced to grave-robbing. St Thomas suggests, timidly, that the angels used compressed air as the material of these bodies. He was, of course, only guessing."

"Gabriel was not out of breath on his arrival in Nazareth."

■

Jacob Delafon has been told, and accepts, that we (he, i.e., human beings) can have no part in the creation of angels.

He assumes that we (he, humanity in general) were created in order that we might fall—perhaps at a moment when reality was in desperate need of history.

In spite of which, he has never been able quite to accept the notion of *æons advancing*.

■

Jacob Delafon reads somewhere, confirming his long held opinion, that angels are not to be trusted.

■

Jacob Delafon turns the hour hand of his watch back one number, to standard time, a transition which, this year, falls oddly on Halloween.

Jacob hates daylight-saving time. He thinks daylight should be squandered.

SKETCH

a sympathetic
tree among ragged
bushes

feathery
leaves and pubescent
stems

floored by that
and

so we are

Jacob Delafon is not sure what life thinks of him, but supposes it must be used to him.

■

Someone yells at Jacob Delafon from a passing car as Jacob navigates the sidewalk: *"Get a haircut, y'queer bastard!"*

Jacob has never thought of his liking women or his having been conceived in wedlock as particularly positive, but something in the tone of voice tells him the rapidly tossed message was meant as an insult.

His hair, he considers, is falling out fast enough and needs no help.

■

Jacob Delafon, after a glance into Nietzsche, asks himself: am I Apollo or am I Bacchus? do I dream or am I drunk?

■

Jacob Delafon loves thunder, but is afraid of lightning. Thus the terrors of the storm are real to him, sublime only in their aftertaste.

Sometimes he wishes he could speak more like thunder. Unsure, in that case, what he would have to say.

■

Jacob Delafon marvels at the idea of a lake lost under a shell of ice, whether in Antarctica or on a moon of Jupiter's.

It makes him think of eyes moving under closed lids, uncertain where sun or where shadow is.

He cannot escape the idea that those lakes dream dreams of falling rain and rising vapor above their crystal prison.

He finds a sentence he has copied out but cannot place, and doesn't know what to make of: "Nothing on earth can harm you, for you are like all things and nothing is unlike you."

■

But Jacob Delafon remembers also some old theologian's

claim that what the light reveals to our eyes can only be our unlikeness.

■

Jacob Delafon, leafing through the *Arcana*, sees that Swedenborg found heaven, in respect to landscape, much like earth. That is, heaven has rivers, has mountains and plains, dry ground and ocean.

Jacob is surprised, since so many others of that time, learned men and visionaries, conceived of this planet, before the Fall, as a perfect sphere—smooth, regular, uniform—its surface torn and wrinkled only by the sin of our unfortunate first parents or (a more scientific view) by the waters of the Flood.

Meanwhile, in every garden, allegories flourish, hyperbolic flowers of burgeoning theory.

■

Jacob Delafon likes to think of things in pairs: high and low, big and little, Mutt and Jeff, life and death, contagious and sympathetic, endocrine and peptide, Ungrund and Umwelt, aromatic rings and buckyballs ...

■

Jacob Delafon has heard that scientific theories—statements involving the structure of the world—are judged, not only for consistency, but also for their formal elegance, for in fact a kind of beauty.

Jacob is bemused, the world, as he knows it, beautiful only in exceptions—only in its inconsistencies.

■

Jacob Delafon has never accepted the formula, *Whatever is, is right.*

Even *Whatever is, is,* seems to him less than certain.

■

Jacob Delafon ponders Noah's ark.

Could it not, after all, have accommodated two giants, male and female?

And does the vastness of time not include, in narrow paths within or beside it, damp forecast of eternity?

SHAPES

dawn—sunset

on—off

oscillatory organization, some kind of
living hourglass

sex—death—leprosy

sensitive surface and
underneath

a silence, brief
but intense

from the heart re-
distributed, curious

ordinary
mind, arbitrary
at the core

imprinted on the
fingers, the whole
animal suffering

under the great ellipses, magnetic
core, do the immortals
dream?

fire—sun—evaporation of car-
bonic acid

ladder to the wall, come

Jacob Delafon reads, in a popular book on cosmology, of a way of graphing reality in which a single point can represent *our entire physical system*, "including the instantaneous motions of all of its parts."

He reads, later in the day, a set of vulgar affirmations presented as theological principles.

Jacob is suspicious of any tone that brings its whole room in with it.

■

". . . modern cosmologists have confirmed that spacetime"—Jacob Delafon, not sure exactly what spacetime is, reads on—spacetime "is flat."

After a moment of puzzlement, he comes to like the idea, finding it thrilling to contemplate living in two dimensions, without giving up his confidence in finding still what he loves, chimneys and fountains, lumps, bumps, filaments.

■

Jacob Delafon has nightmares, but his real terror is not the nightmare dream, nor the night fiend that fetches him nightmares. His terror is the night.

■

Jacob Delafon tries to understand the phrase, "instantaneous motions."

■

Jacob Delafon finds one rope broken, the other intact, the sash hard to manage but able, at certain heights, to be wedged open.

Precariously—on occasion it comes crashing down.

The screen, if he looks at it—unfocusing a gray day—appears to have been attacked by a small animal. Probably it was. The cluster of little rents in the lower mesh was there when he moved in.

And out that same window, behind his house, decades ago, the sycamore had already spread its branches …

■

Though it was by accident that Jacob Delafon, striking

by reflex, has killed a butterfly, he registers the act as his tribute to chaos.

■

"Out of mind," Jacob Delafon thinks, "out of sight."

He passes, thus, unseeing, dark-robed figures, a girl cowering behind the door, a prophet in some other country, the best minds of his generation, some luckless lady or a lackey wandering across the stage, figures falling, fleeing figures, two witnesses and thirteen apparitions, seven hills, a garden of righteousness, tall mortuary candles, drifting continents, stars of gold, the face of the deep.

■

In long fictions, Jacob Delafon concludes, more things ought to be forgotten, like the red shoes of the Duchess.

■

Jacob Delafon reads, attentively, "The Genesis of the Cat's Response to the Rat" by Zing Yang Kuo (1930).

Actually, what he reads, attentively, is a summary of this long article.

Kittens raised in a rat-killing environment, he learns, often turned out to be rat-killers.

Kittens raised in isolation sometimes killed rats, but a majority did not.

Killing a larger rat requires an older and larger cat.

"Vegetarianism had no effect on rat-killing, but had effect on rat-eating."

"The cat is a small-sized tiger."

"Do we need to add that in our findings the cat shows instincts of rat-killing and rat-eating as well as the instinct to love the rat?"

■

Whatever other distinctions might be claimed by the famous Murr, Jacob Delafon takes note that he must be the only tom cat on record with a coat of three colors.

■

For Jacob Delafon, names determine character. For instance, his own first name—from whence his fascination with ladders and with angels.

■

Jacob Delafon tries to stay out of the sun, which—as he says—bangs its light at him.

Whenever possible, he takes shelter.

Shade is his element.

■

Would it be possible, Jacob Delafon wonders—a query with, he supposes, no personal, that is, no practical, application—in, for instance, the polar glare, to be afflicted simultaneously with frostbite and sunburn?

■

This reminds Jacob Delafon of childhood friends he has for long not thought of, remembered now for a sort of game they played. The point was to pair diseases in the worst possible combination.

He does not remember his own contribution to the problem, remembers in fact only one answer—from whom, he has no memory.

But according to this lost juvenile authority, the worst ills to have together, both at once, would be sea-sickness and lockjaw.

■

Dim, caught in the past, stationary, there is—says Jacob Delafon—another sun.

And a future sun as well, trembling with weird beams— retrograde, hypothetical—sliding Jacobwards.

Three suns.

Three sources of shadow.

Deliver me, he prays—to No One—*from their shining*.

■

What, Jacob Delafon wonders, could have been that "strange fire" offered by Aaron's sons? And why did the Lord so despise it?

And he would like to know more about Aaron's "curious girdle."

■

And Inanna. She wanders over the earth, city by city, surrounded by the dead.

Does she still wander? Is she, as Jacob Delafon imagines her, still naked? He is not sorry that her dénouement is lost.

■

Seeing rings in ears, nose, lip, tongue, belly-button, Jacob Delafon, in spite of himself, sometimes wonders what other parts are pierced.

■

Jacob Delafon tries to imagine what trousers the Medes wore, to visualize Babylonian tapestries, to understand sacrificial practice among the Aryans.

He manages sometimes to feel himself surrounded by a garden paradise, canals watering the grass in the meadows, where trees of every species bend verdant boughs over Cyrus' last resting-place.

Jacob would rather like to be felled by an obscure queen.

He would like to humiliate certain gods.

His preparations for founding an empire would include precise and elaborate plans for a glorious tomb.

■

Jacob Delafon tries to understand the notion of sacrifice. He meditates the death of a pig, a mouse, a horse, a dog, slays imaginary children in secret places, in valleys, under rocks, among the smooth stones of the stream.

Sweet scent he finds hard to come by. Burnt meat fills the kitchen with terrible smoke, sharp and harsh and unpleasantly pungent.

Acrid. Irritating.

Corrosive.

Heave offering brings Jacob no peace, nor offering waved anyhow.

AFTERTASTE

half-unawakened

lost word

absorption of light and
scattering

startling
and

the place

this is how it
happens, every
night a little weaker

dreams of uncertain etymology

Believers besiege Jacob Delafon, entreating him to believe. But when he hears a fervent *I believe*, it always seems to him to indicate a hope, a determination, a claim, to believe—to say, in other words, quite clearly: *I do not believe*. Even, in many cases, *If I can get you to believe, I might be able to believe also!*

■

Jacob Delafon comes to realize that any system of belief requires a fund of energy to maintain it.

And to create a system, he decides, would require suspension of belief.

■

Only if something matters, thinks Jacob Delafon, can we search for it.

We can find it, he strongly suspects, only if it does not matter.

■

Jacob Delafon notes that Stefan Themerson classified the expression "good God" as an oxymoron.

Themerson, so far as Jacob remembers, never claimed there is no god, only that there is no god *to speak of*.

■

Everything. Jacob Delafon, opening the *Tractatus*, thinks he perhaps understands this far.

What he cannot quite identify is *the case*.

■

Jacob Delafon would like to bring *know* and *think* closer together, if only to fulfill certain small desires.

■

Some scorpions have twelve eyes, but their vision is poor.

Lice have no wings and no metamorphosis. Their body is so flat that back comes close to belly.

The bedbug likewise: no metamorphosis, no wings. The nymph takes a meal of blood before each moult.

A scorpion was likely the first terrestrial animal.

Jacob Delafon wishes he had studied zoology.

■

Jacob Delafon buys a Camembert in the Sunday market (soft, it seems just ready to eat) and takes it directly home. Unwrapped it has the right smell and color, but as his knife goes in, it begins to writhe, a mass of short well nourished worms.

Were they, he wonders, attracted to this particular cheese because it is exactly their color? Or are they that color, that exact shade, because they have fed on this Camembert?

■

Jacob Delafon likes to quote scripture. To a business man he knows, for instance, he cries,

"Let thy companies deliver thee."

■

Jacob Delafon cannot remember where he read the warning

KEEP OUT OF REACH OF CHILDREN

but he has done his best always.

■

Jacob Delafon finds an old manuscript, torn, covered with mildew. The text begins, "We see clearly ..."

The rest is illegible.

■

Jacob Delafon remembers how, for a while, it was hard to find things. Now he finds it hard to remember what he was looking for.

■

Jacob Delafon has noticed that what he sees (hears, touches ...) does not necessarily matter to him, that few objects in his perceptual range either excite or depress, or in any way move him. That, furthermore, how things do affect him (as they sometimes do) doesn't always relate very firmly to just what it is that he is seeing, hearing, touching. That is to say, there is, of course, the *thing*— but then there's the thing's *feel*, which somehow, sooner or later (in memory perhaps) seems to separate, to detach.

He intones, to himself, silently,

Thirteen apparitions have I seen …

while draping his neutral coat over a harmless hanger.

■

The soul, Smurfit says, is simply appetite.

Jacob Delafon finds this idea satisfying.

But sometimes, after a successful dinner, in persistent reverie, he compares himself to the wild ass, replete with grass, still, at some urge from reason or drive, braying.

■

Jacob Delafon prays (to No One):

"Give us insistence of distance."

"Save us from the rapture of the deep."

■

Jane Floodcab, finding Jacob, as is not infrequent, preoccupied, is wont to fling herself at him, crying out,

"Here I come, body or not."

DISTANCE

afterthought [Nachdenken] re-
tracing and reproducing sub-
merged thought

for example, seeing a category or
just a cat, back and forth, between
maps, quantum-entailed

dead-end, in a series

water-carrier in Hades

we might have met

Jacob Delafon, all his life, has hoped for a mirage. He feels cheated, now, never having found anything but an actual world.

■

"Why is it that bare feet are not good for sexual intercourse?"

"Why are men less capable of sexual intercourse in water?"

"Why is it that, if a living creature is born from our semen, we regard it as our own offspring, but if it proceeds from any other part or excretion, we do not consider it our own?"

"Why are those lustful whose eyelashes fall out?"

Jacob Delafon thinks Aristotle had problems.

"Why does tension and swelling of the penis occur? Is it because it is raised by the weight behind the testicles—the testicles acting as a fulcrum?"

■

Jacob Delafon hesitates uncertainly between position and detachment.

He would balk at descending to some lower level of being—not certain what level that would be.

A glimpse of the divine incomprehensibility seems unrewarding. And the sun hurts Jacob's eyes.

Even so, it sometimes dawns on him that he is holding his head, without conscious purpose, at a tilt.

■

Jacob Delafon hears tell of an animal with two heads. The two heads quarrel violently over which mouth gets certain tidbits, though all the food they devour ends in a common gut.

■

Jacob Delafon is puzzled by the phrase "repeat performance." He thinks of all performance as rehearsal. Rehearsal, to be sure, for No Performance.

■

Jacob Delafon ponders the necessity of material existence.

He picks up a good book, badly printed.

■

The wall in Jacob Delafon's dream, distinct, is a high wall of stone—limestone—dark grey, blank, the rough hewn slabs of stone held together by swallow-tail cramps of lead or iron.

When he dreams, as like anyone he does, he would like to dream a shadowy world.

He would much prefer ridges covered with forest, a gulley of eroded particles, even a steep-sided cleft. Anything to forestall the problem of observation.

Flowers. Lawn. A fountain.

Pavilions of catalpa.

Where he could perfect the art of hiding.

Other lands, with other tongues—memory uninvolved. (Anamnesia: hereditary curse.)

(Independent reality, the mouth or its multiple.)

A margin without a focus, a shadowing forth, a chain of infection, a thing to disappear.

■

Louvre, Jacob Delafon is told, means "place of wolves."

■

Jacob Delafon is asked to picture a clockface. He represents it as the circle described by a sling's rotation.

His sling has no set target, no privileged zone, no firm persuasion.

Asked to explain why the hands come back to where they started, his mind wanders to the islands of an archipelago.

■

Jacob Delafon, finding Jane Floodcab asleep, her breath drawn in and expelled at length, is almost to kiss her, but does not, for fear of waking her. And, besides, her hand is across her mouth.

47

■

Jacob Delafon would rename Jane Floodcab, rename her perhaps continually, a different name for each room she is in—renaming himself as well.

For this, he would prefer common nouns, by singular use made proper.

ARCHIPELAGO

when rain arrives
the candle flame shivers
I have a habit of nothing

a charmed
life and a dozen
wounds
my blankets

when the train arrives
machine out of order
mind deranged
stomach upset
bowels loose
on that day I had not been asleep

support for a god or
perch for a bird
while
behind
time slides by

Jacob Delafon, looking down, sees hard-edged shadows, distinct patches of dark earth, below the most tenuous wisps of cloud, hovering in thin air.

■

Jacob Delafon thinks someone near him is asking, "What is time?" But the answer he hears is, "Half-past three."

■

Dress warmly, Karl.

Clean your room every week.

Wash yourself at least once a week from head to toe.

Use a great big sponge.

Obey your dear father.

Since Jacob Delafon has no mother, he finds maternal letters such as this touching.

■

Jacob Delafon finds words in a French–English diction-
ary that he thinks might someday come in handy, e.g.,

avoir l'œil américain to be wide-awake

se croire sorti de la cuisse de Jupiter to think no
small beer of oneself

mirobolé flabbergasted

mitte ammoniacal exhalation from cesspool

je l'emmène à la campagne! I don't care what he says

c'est pain bénit it serves him right

canard privé stool pigeon

jusqu'à Saint-Glinglin world without end

■

Jacob Delafon would like to construct some small object:
a doll perhaps, or a toy car, or a parallelepipedic box.
What he actually starts to build is a miniature staircase.

But when, after some time, it remains unfinished, he makes many excuses.

Because, he says, it's too big.

Because, he says, it's so far away.

Because it slides.

Because the table isn't soft.

And, anyway, he would rather build a road going down a hill.

Adding, if asked:

A constantly sloping road, supported by pillars of decreasing height.

■

Jacob Delafon lives (lives, that is, part of his time—a small but significant part) among vast phrases, rich eternities.

■

Jacob Delafon cannot help thinking of Blake whenever he feels in his shoe a grain of sand.

■

The idea of a Book of Life is, for Jacob Delafon, ambiguous. It might contain the names of the elect, i.e., those headed for heaven. Or, then again, it might simply list those of us who, now, draw vulgar breath.

■

Beauty (short-range to long), swiftness, the side of a mountain (in movement), strength, reconciliation between effort and repose, liberty, health, pleasure, life everlasting.

Jacob Delafon, unable to keep in mind these various benefits to the risen elect, looks them up again. But, as so often, he cannot keep his mind on one thing.

■

Jacob Delafon notes that the punishment of Adam and Eve was not what they had been threatened with: death. Their sentences were, instead, sweat and childbirth. They were condemned to live.

■

Jacob Delafon was impressed, even as a child, by how squirrels avoided him, not by running up a tree, but simply by scrambling to the other side of the trunk, out of his line of sight.

He wonders sometimes what other creatures, what other phenomena, so hide themselves.

■

My love is a red red rose ...

My love is like a red red rose ...

Jacob Delafon cannot see the difference.

■

Jacob Delafon reads of those with unusual powers of memory, or with a lively sense of humor, some making private noise, harassed by too much yin (chills) or too much yang (fever), or poor relations, or problems of erasure, some expecting to sleep until the resurrection, others beset by distressing doubt at Göttingen, or elsewhere, figures in prayer with extended arms, with a look of death, astonished and filthy, in eternal torment, wolves of evening, dawn leopards, anonymous monuments.

He is addicted to biography.

∎

Jacob Delafon heeds the unknown instructor who declared, "No use having a theory if it tires you."

∎

Intellectually, Jacob Delafon is a splitter. His heart, however, leans towards lumping.

Thus he tends to grind finely and accumulate great awkward piles.

He would like at least to be able to say, "I have made a heap of all that I could find," but in practice he scatters.

∎

If, as Jacob Delafon has read, "Everything is sentient," why, he wonders, is there so little consciousness?

∎

Jacob Delafon, passing the Vedanta Society, notes this week's sermon topic: *Seeing God With Open Eyes*.

Jacob pauses to consider this, having always supposed it more common with eyes closed, usually after a thump on the head.

■

Walking, Jacob Delafon sees messages in the sidewalk, pressed into the cement before it hardened. Crude as the letters are, the words are legible.

"LEGALIZE HEMP," he reads, just across from Starbuck's.

Further on, "PLANT A TREE OR DIE."

■

Jacob Delafon has run across the suggestion (not, he suspects, widely accepted as orthodox) that God did not rest after the Creation, but only after Crucifixion.

■

Jacob Delafon's god has all the attributes ever suggested for deity, except that of "existence."

Jacob's relation to god is not that of believer to being. Nor does it resemble that of artwork to artist, pot to potter.

It is, perhaps, a little like the relation of character to plot.

■

Jacob Delafon dreams of a goddess in the form of a cow. Other deities go flying by: geese, ducks, fowl in general—and finally birds of any and every kind.

Below, on a broad plain, he sees what he takes to be Elephant City, at any rate a place of settled life, ponderous and slow moving.

If he lifts his eyes he catches, fitfully, a glimpse into another dimension: castles of air, cities of fire.

Trapped in his dream, he becomes *the god of the extended arm*.

■

Jacob Delafon is disappointed that three volumes of Jabès were not published by Yale University Press. How marvelous, he thinks, a spine which could read

Yael

Elya

Aely

Yale

■

While reading a book, whose title and author—as well as subject—he has forgotten, Jacob Delafon jotted down, what he tries now to understand:

neighboring river

the liquid that is life

local waters

bathe

fountain-head

abundant liquid

rain

a sapling owes its foliage

springs

concealed rain

deep places of the sea

cutting hair and beard for the dead

it is to the lower jawbone that the ghost attaches itself

the apertures of the house

white tunic, gold trimmed

adding flavor to the landscape

■

Jacob Delafon's friend Mott laments the coming of old age. Jacob—the same age as his friend—insists that he, Jacob, has lost nothing to the years. He was, after all, never bold, never strong, never good looking.

And what could he do, back then, that he can not do now?

True, he concedes, after mature consideration, he can never, now, die young.

■

To his friend Mott, Jacob Delafon claims, perhaps seriously, that the truly fortunate writers of the nineteenth century were John Keats and Emily Brontë.

Mott seems unconvinced.

But yes, says Jacob. Each, hardly adult, produced an absolute masterpiece. *Wuthering Heights*. *The Odes*. And then—then they got the hell out.

■

Jacob Delafon finds in Partridge's dictionary,

shit! mother, I can't dance

which, according to Partridge, means nothing at all, being simply what one says "just for something to say."

■

A bench.

A stool.

A small table.

A bed.

A Bible.

A cow.

Two chairs.

These are not what Jacob Delafon will leave behind.

■

Words fail Jacob Delafon, sometimes refusing to express what he meant to say, more often by saying more than he means.

■

The continents: they are, Jacob Delafon suspects, so many traces of terrestial memory.

He feels himself at times, when past images come unbidden to mind, a creature cast up on a remote shore—or trying to recall a lost notion, he scratches at loose sand in a vain attempt to crawl from a sea indefinite, undefinable.

■

Jacob Delafon reads of an Arabic poetic form called *qasida* — which, according to some ninth century writer, may be about almost anything, but "should begin with the evocation of lost dwelling places and lost love, continue with the description of a journey, and culminate in the real subject."

In fact, the house where Jacob lives, and has lived for years, and where he will continue to live, he considers his lost home; Jane, in his arms, his lost love.

What he cannot seem to get to is a real subject.

■

Jacob Delafon, unaware of his author's hand, covets a complete personality, but exists only in facets.

"I am satisfied," says Jacob, in a phrase lifted from beyond his ken, "*in nothing so much, as in knowing that nothing can satisfie me.*"

■

Jacob Delafon, sometimes, like Coleridge, craves "the flush, the overflow."

■

This isn't, thinks Jacob Delafon, at all what he expected.

Then it occurs to him that he has no idea exactly what it was he expected.

And is not completely sure what "This" refers to.

TO SAY

the capacity
of air, grains of
vapor—that phenomenon the
rainbow

through

clearer air, if a
rain-drop dropping, after

beauty, orna-
mental

ghost
of suspicion, picture

now

yourself at

When Jacob Delafon looks more closely, to his surprise

ABOUT THE AUTHOR

Keith Waldrop co-edits, with Rosmarie Waldrop, the small press Burning Deck, founded in 1961 while they were graduate students at the University of Michigan; he has taught at Brown University since 1968. His first book, *A Windmill Near Calvary*, was nominated for the National Book Award. *The Silhouette of the Bridge*, part of a trilogy published by Avec, won the 1997 Americas Award for Poetry. His translations of contemporary French poetry have been supported by two NEA translation fellowships and the government of France has awarded him the rank of Chevalier des Arts et Lettres.

Library of Congress Cataloging-in-Publication Data

Waldrop, Keith.
 The real subject : queries and conjectures of Jacob Delafon :
with sample poems / poetry by Keith Waldrop.
  p. cm.
 ISBN 1-890650-15-3 (alk. paper)
 I. Title.

 PS3573.A423R43 2004
 811'.54--dc22

                              2004011790